CW01082670

Original title:

Chasing Moonbeams to Dreamland

Copyright © 2024 Creative Arts Management OÜ

All rights reserved.

Author: Colin Leclair

ISBN HARDBACK: 978-9916-90-342-1

ISBN PAPERBACK: 978-9916-90-343-8

Celestial Wanderers Unite

In the vast expanse, they roam free,
Stars that shimmer, wild and carefree.
Galaxies whisper, tales untold,
Bringing dreams, both new and old.

Through cosmic dances, they entwine,
Creating paths, where worlds align.
With constellations as their guide,
In cosmic seas, together they glide.

The Fables of the Silver Sky

Once upon a twilight, stars took flight,
Whispering stories in the night.
Moonbeams gather, secrets unfold,
Tales of glory, waiting to be told.

Each silver glow, a passage through time,
Echoes of laughter, a sweet chime.
Fables of lovers, lost in the glow,
Under the heavens, their hearts aglow.

Reflections in a Moonlit Pool

In silence deep, the water gleams,
Holding secrets, housing dreams.
Moonlight dances on its face,
Time stands still, in this sacred space.

Ripples whisper, stories depart,
Carried softly, they touch the heart.
Each reflected star a wish,
Guiding souls to moments vivid and swish.

The Night's Celestial Playground

Amidst the shadows, laughter rings,
In the playground where starlight sings.
Galaxies swirl, in playful embrace,
A cosmic carnival, a wondrous place.

Nebulas bloom, like flowers bright,
In this realm of shimmering night.
Every twinkle a joyful cheer,
As the universe joins in, ever near.

Serene Slumbers Beneath the Moon

Soft whispers cradle the night,
A blanket of stars, silver bright.
Dreams woven gently with care,
In serene slumbers, free from despair.

Moonlight dances on the ground,
In the stillness, peace is found.
Crickets sing a lullaby tune,
While we drift, beneath the moon.

Dreamscapes in Ethereal Glow

Colors swirl in twilight's grace,
Through dreamscapes vast, we softly trace.
Whispers of magic softly call,
In realms where time does not enthrall.

Floating on clouds of shimmering light,
Adventures await in the heart of night.
In this ethereal glow we roam,
Finding our way, we are never alone.

The Night's Dreamcatcher

A web of stars catches the dreams,
Sewn with laughter, stitched with beams.
In the darkness, shadows play,
While the night whispers, come what may.

Each breath a secret, soft and light,
The dreamcatcher guards through the night.
With each prayer, a wish takes flight,
In the embrace of the silent night.

Phantoms of the Midnight Breeze

Phantoms dance in shadows deep,
Carried on winds that softly sweep.
Through the trees, a haunting sigh,
As secrets of the night draw nigh.

Whispers echo, tales unfold,
Of memories wrapped in silver and gold.
The midnight breeze, a gentle guide,
In its embrace, the dreams abide.

Odyssey of the Star Gazers

Under the vast celestial dome,
Whispers pull at dreams to roam.
In the night, our spirits soar,
Searching for what lies in store.

Galaxies dance in velvet hues,
Each twinkle tells of ancient views.
Hands extend to touch the night,
Holding on to distant light.

Adventures borne on cosmic winds,
Where time and space begin and blend.
Lost in realms of endless sight,
We chase the trails of starlit night.

The Twilight Whisper of Fantasies

As twilight drapes the world in gold,
Secrets of dreams begin to unfold.
Soft melodies in shadows play,
Inviting thoughts to drift away.

In the hush, where hopes ignite,
Fantasies dance in soft twilight.
Colors blend in splendid grace,
Imagination finds its place.

Stories brewed in evening air,
Magic blooms without a care.
Every whisper, every sigh,
Echoes of the day gone by.

Voyage Through Celestial Dreams

On a ship of silver and gold,
We sail where the dreams unfold.
Stars are our compass, guiding true,
Through realms of lavender and blue.

In the realm where wishes fly,
Clouds are pillows in the sky.
Every wave tells tales of old,
Of treasures hidden, truths untold.

Each heartbeat syncs with cosmic flow,
In the dreamscape, we gently row.
With every star, our hopes ascend,
To find the wonders without end.

Reflections on the Silver Tides

Moonlit waters, calm and clear,
Reflect the dreams that bring us near.
Gentle ripples, whispers glide,
Carrying secrets with the tide.

Glistening beneath the cosmic light,
Waves carry echoes of the night.
Memories drift like boats at sea,
Embracing all that's yet to be.

Time flows softly, like the sand,
In the stillness, we take a stand.
With every tide, we find our way,
Guided by the stars' soft sway.

The Moonlit Canvas of Possibility

Under a sky of silver glow,
Dreams dance softly, breathless flow.
Stars whisper secrets, old yet new,
A canvas wide, inviting you.

With every brush of night's embrace,
Life unfolds in gentle grace.
Colors shimmer, time held still,
Painting visions, hearts to fill.

In shadows deep, adventure gleams,
A world reborn in silent dreams.
Each stroke tells tales yet untold,
A moonlit magic, pure and bold.

Possibilities stretch and sway,
In this realm where spirits play.
Let your heart, like comets, soar,
On this canvas, forevermore.

Constellations of Unseen Realms

Beneath the stars, we close our eyes,
Seeking truths beyond the skies.
Constellations whisper far and near,
Of hidden realms, they beckon clear.

In twilight's glow, the echoes rise,
Stories linger, lost in sighs.
Galaxies spin in timeless flight,
Guiding souls through endless night.

Beyond the veil, the shadows play,
Mysteries wrapped in the moon's sway.
Each twinkle holds a whispered call,
Unseen realms, we yearn to know them all.

With every heartbeat, we align,
In cosmic dance, our fates entwine.
The universe speaks in gentle streams,
Where dreams converge in starlit beams.

Glimmering Shores of Nighttime Dreams

Waves of silver kiss the shore,
Whispers echo, longing for more.
Underneath a tapestry spun,
Nighttime dreams begin to run.

Each grain of sand holds a wish,
In twilight's embrace, hearts can swish.
Glimmering paths of moonlit rays,
Guide us through our nightly maze.

Ebbing tides sing lullabies,
Underneath the starry skies.
Dreams unfurl like sails on seas,
Carried along on midnight breeze.

In this realm where shadows play,
Hope and magic softly sway.
Glimmering shores, our hearts ignite,
In dreams that flourish through the night.

The Haunting Call of the Nocturne

In the silence of the night,
Notes of haunting take their flight.
An echo calls from deep within,
Where shadows dance and souls begin.

Melodies weave through sacred air,
Carrying whispers, soft and rare.
The noontide fades, the moon ascends,
A serenade that never ends.

With every chord, the heart takes wing,
In night's embrace, it learns to sing.
The haunting call of dreams awake,
Echoing through each breath we take.

In twilight's calm, we find our way,
Guided by music's soft ballet.
The noontide's whisper lingers near,
A timeless song, forever clear.

A Voyage through the Infinite Sky

Upon the wings of silver light,
We soar through dreams both day and night.
A tapestry of stars unfolds,
Where secrets of the cosmos hold.

Through cosmic seas, we drift and glide,
Past moons and comets, side by side.
Each twinkle sings a song of old,
Of journeys brave and tales retold.

With every breath, the stardust flows,
In endless realms where wonder grows.
The universe, a vast embrace,
In timeless depths, we find our place.

As we traverse this boundless space,
We leave behind the earthly race.
A voyage forever intertwined,
In cosmic winds, our souls unwined.

The Sway of Ethereal Whispers

In the hush of twilight's breath,
Whispers dance, and shadows heft.
The breeze carries secrets sweet,
Of hidden realms where spirits meet.

Silken strands of mist entwine,
In gentle curves, the stars align.
Each note a promise softly spun,
In the heart of night, two souls are one.

Cascading echoes in the dark,
Illuminate a sacred spark.
Awakening dreams that softly sway,
Guiding hearts that long to play.

Through the veil of time we glide,
In ethereal realms where hopes abide.
With every whisper, we explore,
The magic found forevermore.

Harbor of Celestial Fantasies

Where the oceans kiss the stars,
A harbor waits with dreams from far.
Waves of light on shores of grace,
Ebb and flow in a timeless space.

Sails adorned with wishes bright,
Catch the currents of the night.
In this haven, love blooms free,
As stardust mingles with the sea.

Mysteries lie beneath the veil,
In every wind, a whispered tale.
Set your course for shores unknown,
In this celestial realm, we've grown.

Together, we cast nets of dreams,
Where the universe always seems,
To cradle hearts in soft embrace,
In the harbor's warm, inviting space.

Escapades in Dreamstruck Meadows

In meadows lush, where wildflowers play,
We dance beneath the sun's soft ray.
Each petal whispers tales of old,
In vibrant hues, our dreams unfold.

Laughter echoes through the air,
As breezes twirl beyond compare.
Here in this realm of endless bliss,
Every moment, a stolen kiss.

Butterflies flit with graceful ease,
As hearts embrace a gentle breeze.
We wander paths of golden light,
In dreamstruck meadows, pure delight.

With every step, the world transforms,
In magic spun from nature's charms.
Together we chase the daylight's gleam,
In the essence of a waking dream.

The Dance of Lunar Light

Beneath the moon's soft glow,
Shadows sway and flicker,
Stars twirl in the night sky,
As whispers of dreams linger.

Silver beams from high above,
Guide the heart in stillness,
While the world breathes its sigh,
Wrapped in lunar brilliance.

Each star a twinkling wish,
In patterns that softly move,
The night a great ballet,
In light that seems to groove.

As silence takes its place,
In this celestial sphere,
The dance of life unfolds,
With every twinkling tear.

Starlit Pathways to Enchantment

Along the paths of silver light,
Journeys weave like dreams,
Guiding souls with gentle might,
Through realms of other themes.

Each step a rhythmic pulse with fate,
While shadows softly hum,
The night alive with tales of late,
In the dark, we become.

Whispers float on midnight breeze,
Secrets of the night laid bare,
The starlit pathways, wild and free,
Invite us to their lair.

In every twinkling eye we see,
An invitation to explore,
The magic woven endlessly,
On starlit paths and more.

Echoes of Nocturnal Dreams

In the hush of night's embrace,
Where shadows softly sigh,
Echoes dance in sacred space,
Beneath the velvet sky.

Dreams awaken at this hour,
Carried on the breeze,
With every star, a hidden power,
Whispers in the trees.

Nocturnal wonders come alive,
As eyes begin to close,
The heartbeats gently strive,
To follow where it goes.

In echoes find the truth we seek,
In whispers find our way,
The night invites the bold, the meek,
To dance 'til break of day.

Adventures in the Night Sky

High above, the sky ignites,
With colors pure and bright,
Each star a tale of daring flights,
In the canvas of the night.

Galaxies swirl in cosmic spree,
A dance of dreams and chance,
Adventure waits for you and me,
In this celestial dance.

Planets whisper secrets old,
In orbits wide and true,
Every wanderer shall behold,
The wonders just for you.

So let us soar through starry seas,
On wings of our delight,
Embrace the night, the mysteries,
In adventures of pure light.

Radiance Beyond the Horizon

A dawn that breaks with golden light,
Caressing skies in hues so bright.
The whispers of the morning breeze,
Awakening the world with ease.

Mountains stand in silent grace,
Holding secrets in their embrace.
The sun ascends, a fiery sphere,
Chasing shadows, casting fear.

Rivers glisten, dancing free,
Reflecting all their harmony.
Nature sings in joyful rhyme,
A symphony within the climb.

As day unfolds with fervent glow,
Hope ignites in hearts below.
The horizon stretches, wide and vast,
With radiance that's unsurpassed.

Woven Threads of Midnight's Embrace

In the quiet of the night,
Stars weave tales of pure delight.
Threads of silver in the dark,
Each a story, each a spark.

Moonlight dances on the ground,
Casting shadows all around.
Whispers soft like gentle streams,
Echo softly through our dreams.

Velvet skies and endless space,
Nature's calm, a warm embrace.
In stillness, hearts begin to soar,
Finding peace forevermore.

Time dissolves, a fleeting breath,
In midnight's arms, we tease with death.
Awake, alive with thoughts unspoken,
A world reborn, no line unbroken.

Whispers of Silvery Shadows

Beneath the trees where secrets dwell,
Silvery shadows weave their spell.
Whispers float upon the breeze,
Carrying tales through ancient leaves.

Moonbeams touch the forest floor,
Illuminating dreams of yore.
In the hush of twilight's sigh,
Mysteries gather, drawing nigh.

Echoes of the past entwined,
In every rustle, voices find.
Stories shared through ages long,
In the dark, we hear their song.

As night descends and stars align,
We feel the pulse of the divine.
In the shadows, our fears erase,
Finding solace in their grace.

A Journey Through Starlit Veils

Step softly on the cosmic path,
Where dreams and wonders intertwine.
Every star a guiding light,
Illuminating hearts so bright.

Veils of night, a tapestry,
Woven with threads of mystery.
Each twinkle tells a tale profound,
In this vast space, life is found.

Galaxies swirl in harmony,
A dance of fate, a symphony.
As we wander through the skies,
Infinite wonders greet our eyes.

Across the realms of dusk and dawn,
Lost in time, yet never gone.
A journey not of maps and goals,
But of the spirit, and of souls.

The Moon's Gentle Lullaby

In the night, the moonlight glows,
Whispers soft like velvet flows.
Dreams take flight on silver beams,
Resting hearts in quiet dreams.

Breezes weave through midnight trees,
Carrying sweet, serene decrees.
Stars above twinkle with ease,
Lulling whispers in the breeze.

Clouds drift by in silken shrouds,
Silence wraps the sleeping crowds.
Time slows down, the world a sigh,
Underneath the watchful sky.

Crickets sing in harmony,
Nature's tune, a symphony.
Close your eyes, and drift away,
In the arms of night, we stay.

Secrets of the Cosmic Sea

Waves of stardust gently roll,
Whispers of the universe's soul.
Each pint of light a tale unfolds,
In the depths where wonder molds.

Galaxies swirl like ancient lore,
Hidden shores we can explore.
Nebulas bloom in colors bright,
Painting dreams in cosmic night.

Time and space, they intertwine,
Secrets held in silence divine.
A dance of planets, pure and vast,
Echoes of the future and past.

Beneath the stars, we find our way,
Sailing through the Milky Way.
In the cosmic sea, we're free,
Holding close eternity.

A Voyage on Ethereal Winds

Winds of magic gently blow,
Across the realms where wonders grow.
Kites of dreams in skies we send,
To the horizon, where journeys blend.

Clouds like ships in azure seas,
Carrying hopes upon the breeze.
With each gust, our spirits soar,
A dance of freedom we explore.

Through fields of starlight, we glide,
On ethereal winds, we ride.
Every whisper, each new flight,
Guides us deeper into the night.

Horizons call, adventures gleam,
A tapestry woven with a dream.
Boundless skies, we make our stand,
In this voyage, hand in hand.

Starlit Conversations

Underneath the velvet sky,
Stars converse, as ages fly.
Whispers soft, they drift and sway,
In the night, they share their play.

Every glimmer has a sound,
In this space, the heart is found.
Stories told without a word,
In the silence, thoughts are stirred.

Planets nod in soft reply,
Echoes of the cosmos high.
Dancing lights, our thoughts connect,
In this realm, we all reflect.

Starlit dreams seep into mind,
In this moment, peace we find.
Conversations with the night,
A celestial, endless flight.

Secrets Wrapped in Twilight's Veil

Whispers dance beneath the stars,
As shadows stretch and secrets rise.
The moonlight weaves its silver bars,
Enfolding dreams in twilight's sighs.

Softly, night wraps all in grace,
Where mysteries in silence play.
Each heartbeat time cannot erase,
In twilight's arms we gently sway.

Beneath the cloak of dusky shade,
Truths hidden, long kept at bay.
In every glimmer, hopes are made,
As night unveils what dreams convey.

Fantasies on a Silver Horizon

On silver shores where dreams collide,
The ocean calls with whispered schemes.
With every wave, our hearts abide,
In fantasies entwined with beams.

Clouds of hope float soft and light,
As sunlight kisses ocean's foam.
A dance of joy in colors bright,
Where every heart can find a home.

With every tide, a tale unfolds,
Of love and laughter, sweet and true.
In silver echoes, bold and bold,
We chase the magic, me and you.

Glimmers of Hope in the Dark

In shadows deep where silence creeps,
A flicker glows with tender grace.
For those who seek where sadness weeps,
Hope lights the path, a warm embrace.

Stars pierce the void, a gentle spark,
Each glimmer tells a story new.
Through darkest nights, we find the arc,
Of dreams that whisper, 'You will do.'

When heavy hearts feel all alone,
In quiet moments, courage blooms.
With glimmers bright, no fear can own,
Our spirits rise above the glooms.

The Lanterns of Lost Dreams

Upon the path where hopes once stood,
Lanterns flicker, soft and low.
Each light a wish wrapped in its wood,
In memory's glow, the past will flow.

When night descends, and stars take flight,
The lanterns guide our weary hearts.
In every beam, there shines a light,
To remind us of life's arts.

Through shadows deep and winding ways,
We hold these lights with tender care.
For in lost dreams, the heart still plays,
With lanterns shining everywhere.

Rhapsody of Stars and Shadows

In the whisper of twilight's embrace,
Shadows dance with a soft, subtle grace.
Stars awaken with a shimmering sigh,
Painting secrets across the darkening sky.

A melody calls from the depths of night,
Echoing dreams that take elegant flight.
With each flicker, a story unfolds,
Ancient tales of the brave and the bold.

Beneath the watchful gaze of the moon,
Hearts stir gently, a sweet, silent tune.
In shadows, we find our spirits set free,
A rhapsody sung by the night's gentle plea.

Together we dance in the soft purple haze,
Lost in the magic of the night's warm embrace.
For in the hours when the stars align,
Shadows and light create a world so divine.

Dreamweaving in Starlit Silence

In the cradle of night, where dreams intertwine,
Starlit whispers weave a tale so divine.
Each flicker a promise, each twinkle a dance,
In silence we float, lost in our trance.

The cosmos hums softly, a lullaby bright,
Guiding our thoughts through the depths of night.
Eyes closed, we wander through realms unseen,
In the heart of the dark, where spirits convene.

Clouds drift like secrets, unraveling slow,
While constellations keep their watch from below.
With each gentle heartbeat, we weave our dreams wide,
In starlit silence, let our hopes gently glide.

Together we soar on the wings of the night,
In this tapestry woven from moonbeam light.
For within the stillness, our souls find their way,
In dreams and in shadows, forever we sway.

The Canvas of Night's Imagination

On the canvas of night, colors unfold,
Brushstrokes of wonder, silent and bold.
With stars as our palette, we venture to dream,
In the depth of the dark, where the echoes gleam.

Galaxies twinkle like jewels from afar,
Each forming a picture, a night's shining star.
Clouds drift like whispers, softly they sway,
As our thoughts take flight on the wings of the way.

Painted horizons invite us to see,
Visions of worlds that could one day be.
With each passing moment, the night blooms anew,
A canvas of dreams in the midnight hue.

In the silence of dusk, imagination flies,
With each brush of a star, let our spirits rise.
For on the canvas of night, we create and explore,
A masterpiece born at the heavens' door.

When Night Meets the Horizon

When night meets the horizon, a journey begins,
The sky cradles lost dreams, where silence spins.
Stars flicker softly, whispering low,
Secrets of shadows where soft breezes flow.

As darkness unfolds like a blanket of peace,
The world takes a breath, finding gentle release.
With horizons ablaze, horizons of fire,
In the heart of the night, the soul lifts higher.

In twilight's embrace, we seek what's unseen,
Where dusk kisses dawn, a magical sheen.
With each passing moment, the colors collide,
As dreams from the shadows and light coincide.

Thus, when night meets the horizon's soft glow,
We journey together where wild rivers flow.
In the dance of the dark, a story ignites,
When night meets the horizon, we embrace the sights.

Serenade of Infinite Stars

In the quiet of night sky,
The stars begin to play,
Whispers of dreams aloft,
Guiding the hearts that sway.

Each twinkle tells a tale,
Of hopes and wishes cast,
A melody of light,
In the vastness unsurpassed.

The moon, a silver muse,
Dances on the sea,
While shadows gently hum,
To the rhythm of the free.

Hearts lift like the breeze,
With every twinkling glance,
A serenade of love,
In a cosmic, timeless dance.

When the Night Calls

When the night calls softly,
With secrets wrapped in air,
Voices of the dusky deep,
Draw me in their snare.

Stars like lanterns flicker,
Guiding lost souls home,
In the embrace of shadows,
No more do they roam.

The moon, a watchful guardian,
Bathe us in its glow,
Timeless whispers linger,
In the night's gentle flow.

Silent dreams awaken,
With each lingering sigh,
In the symphony of stillness,
Where time dares not to fly.

Enigmatic Sojourns of the Heart

In the labyrinth of feeling,
Where shadows weave and twist,
The heart embarks on journeys,
Across a moonlit mist.

Every sigh a mystery,
Every tear a song,
In the depths of longing,
Where we know we belong.

Emotions like a river,
Flowing wild and free,
Each turn a revelation,
In love's deep tapestry.

Daylight may seem fleeting,
But night holds us tight,
In these enigmatic sojourns,
Our spirits take their flight.

Floating on Gossamer Clouds

Floating on gossamer clouds,
Where dreams begin to soar,
Each fluffy wisp a promise,
Of lands we've yet to explore.

With hearts as light as feathers,
We dance on softest air,
A world of golden sunlight,
Where every joy we share.

Beneath a sky so endless,
We weave our tales of light,
In the whispers of the breeze,
Our spirits take their flight.

Together we are drifting,
In the warmth of gentle beams,
Floating on gossamer clouds,
Lost in the arms of dreams.

Wandering Through Silver Mists

Through silver mists, the path unfolds,
Where whispers of the night are told.
Each step embraced by shadows' grace,
I lose myself in this timeless space.

The moonlight dances on the ground,
In silver beams, a soft surround.
The world awakes, yet dreams still cling,
In this serene and haunting spring.

With every breath, a story flows,
Of silent woods and secret throes.
The gentle night, a tender guide,
Through silver mist, I here reside.

Yet with the dawn, I must take flight,
As colors burst, dispelling night.
Yet in my heart, those mists shall stay,
A haunting dream that won't decay.

The Secret Garden of Twilight

In twilight's glow, we find our place,
A garden hidden, trimmed with grace.
Where flowers bloom in shades of night,
And secrets thrive away from sight.

The gentle breeze, a tender kiss,
Awakens dreams we dare not miss.
Each petal holds a whispered lore,
Of love and loss, and so much more.

The stars above like jewels gleam,
In this enchanted, quiet dream.
Here in the hush, our spirits soar,
Through twilight paths forevermore.

Within this garden, time suspends,
As nature sighs and softly blends.
Our hearts entwined, we linger long,
In twilight's arms, we are both strong.

Celestial Trails of Wonder

Upon the night, the stars align,
A tapestry of fate divine.
Each twinkle tells of dreams pursued,
In celestial trails of gratitude.

With stardust drifting through the air,
We chase our hopes, no room for fear.
As constellations guide our way,
In cosmic realms, we long to stay.

The universe, a vast embrace,
Reveals the mysteries we chase.
With every heartbeat, we ascend,
On trails of wonder, without end.

With comet tails that streak the skies,
We gather strength, we dare to rise.
In unity, our spirits beam,
Bound by the light of every dream.

Embracing the Lunar Embrace

In shadows deep, the moon's caress,
A silver touch, a soft confess.
With gentle beams, it warms my soul,
In lunar light, I feel made whole.

The night unfolds, a velvet sheet,
Where dreams and silence dance and meet.
Each star above, a watchful eye,
As nightingale songs fill the sky.

With every phase, a promise sworn,
In tender glow, my heart reborn.
I seek the wisdom moonbeams share,
In silent truths, the world laid bare.

So let me dwell beneath this light,
Embracing all that feels so right.
In lunar arms, my spirit flies,
A tranquil heart that never lies.

Beneath the Veil of Night

The moon whispers secrets soft,
As shadows dance on silent ground.
Stars twinkle like distant dreams,
In the embrace of night profound.

Whispers of the midnight breeze,
Carry tales of time gone by.
With every rustle of the leaves,
The world sighs a gentle sigh.

Beneath this cloak of velvet dark,
Hearts awaken, desires spark.
In this realm of quiet grace,
Lies the magic we often chase.

So linger here beneath the stars,
Let worries fade and dreams take flight.
For in the peace of night's embrace,
We find our truth, our inner light.

Reveries in Celestial Silence

In the quiet of the void,
Thoughts drift like cosmic dust.
Time flows gently, unalloyed,
In silence, we find our trust.

Galaxies spin in vast array,
Echoes of an ancient song.
Beneath this dome of soft decay,
We weave where we truly belong.

Stars shimmer with forgotten tales,
Of love and loss, of hope and fear.
Each twinkle a whisper that prevails,
In this silence, dreams appear.

So close your eyes and drift away,
To where the universe unfolds.
In reverie, we'll softly sway,
In celestial grace, be consoled.

Riding the Wings of Dreams

On silken breezes we take flight,
Our spirits soar, unchained and free.
Through realms of wonder, pure delight,
On the wings of dreams, we see.

Clouds become our pillows soft,
As we dance on moonlit beams.
With every thought we drift aloft,
In a world that bends to dreams.

Bright hues of dawn paint the sky,
Awakening hopes within our hearts.
In this moment, we shall try,
To seize the day, ignite new starts.

So let us ride the currents high,
Trusting in the paths we choose.
For in our dreams, we'll learn to fly,
And find the life in which we lose.

Silhouettes of Stardust

In twilight's soft embrace we stand,
Silhouettes against the fading light.
Each heartbeat writes a timeless strand,
Crafted in the fabric of night.

Stars brush our dreams with silver lines,
As shadows stretch across the ground.
In this stillness, starlight shines,
In silhouettes, lost hopes are found.

We wander through this astral sea,
Where every gaze ignites a spark.
In whispers shared, there's unity,
Amidst the glow, we leave our mark.

So let the night wrap us in peace,
As stardust lingers in our veins.
Here, in the dark, our souls release,
Finding joy where memory reigns.

Navigating the Dreamy Nebula

In realms where stardust softly glows,
We sail through cosmic tides that flow.
Each spark a tale, a whispered sigh,
Beneath the vast, eternal sky.

Galaxies twirl in dance divine,
Charting paths with hopes entwined.
Nebulae shimmer, colors blend,
In dreams where time and space transcend.

A compass forged from ancient light,
Guides us through the endless night.
With every breath, the universe waits,
For us to unlock its mystic gates.

So hold your dreams, let them unfurl,
In this bright tapestry we twirl.
Together we'll explore the seam,
Navigating this dreamy dream.

Images of the Lunar Woodlands

Beneath the pale and silvered beams,
The woodlands breathe in quiet dreams.
Moonlight drapes on leaves like lace,
In shadows deep, ghosts find their place.

Whispers rustle through the trees,
Carried soft on the evening breeze.
Creatures stir in night's embrace,
Lunar glow their fleeting grace.

Each branch a story, each bark a song,
In the stillness, they hum along.
Cypress towers review the night,
Guarding secrets out of sight.

Images flicker in silver clouds,
Moonlit dances with nature's shrouds.
In this realm, where shadows play,
The heart finds peace, come what may.

Dreams Carried on the Night's Whispers

On the velvet wings of silent nights,
Dreams take flight on starlit heights.
Each whisper weaves a magic tale,
Guiding thoughts on the night's soft sail.

Lingering wishes float like dust,
In the quiet, we place our trust.
The moon gazes with a knowing smile,
As dreams wander free for a while.

Night's breath carries secrets deep,
Cradling dreams as the world sleeps.
Fragments of hope, like glimmering lights,
Shatter darkness and rise to heights.

Awake, yet lost in endless sea,
Each whisper a gentle decree.
Night shall hold what dreams unfold,
In embrace of shadows bold.

Beneath the Twilight Canopy

As sun dips low and shadows grow,
Under twilight's soft, golden glow.
Nature sighs as day takes flight,
In this gentle embrace of night.

Branches arch in graceful arcs,
Whispers float like soft embers' sparks.
The world exhales a peaceful tune,
Beneath the watchful, silvered moon.

Stars emerge through veils of dusk,
Painting skies in hues of musk.
Owls awaken, their watch begun,
In the magic where shadows run.

Here in the dusk, dreams intertwine,
Life pauses under stars that shine.
With every heartbeat, peace takes hold,
Beneath the canopy, a tale unfolds.

Whispers of Silver Light

In the quiet of the night,
Softly glows the silver bright.
Whispers dance on gentle breeze,
Carrying secrets, aiming to please.

Among the trees, a silver sheen,
Illuminates where dreams have been.
Each twinkle holds a hidden thought,
A tapestry of what we sought.

Moonlit paths weave tales untold,
In silver light, the heart grows bold.
Echoes linger, soft and wise,
Guiding us beneath starry skies.

As morning breaks, the whispers fade,
Yet in our hearts, they still cascade.
We hold the night in memories dear,
In silver light, we conquer fear.

Dancing Shadows on Cloud's Edge

Shadows twirl in twilight's glow,
On the brink where dreams may flow.
Clouds like dancers in the sky,
Paint their stories soaring high.

Whispers float on cool night air,
Together twirling without a care.
Every silhouette tells a tale,
Of twilight journeys, soft and pale.

The moonlight casts a gentle path,
Where shadows play, avoiding wrath.
In this realm, all hearts feel free,
Dancing shadows, just you and me.

As night unfolds its velvet cloak,
In each heartbeat, we gently stoke.
Dreams and echoes intertwine,
In this dance, your hand in mine.

Starlit Pathways to Enchantment

Along the starlit pathway glows,
A secret world that softly knows.
Twinkling lights like fireflies,
Guiding souls 'neath endless skies.

Each step whispers a silent song,
Inviting all to join along.
Magic lingers in the night,
Wrapped in dreams and soft moonlight.

Footprints traced with stardust fair,
In this haven, free of care.
Journey deeper, hearts take flight,
On starlit pathways, pure delight.

With every star, a wish does spark,
Illuminating love's true arc.
Together we will find our way,
In enchanted night's embrace we stay.

Where the Nightingale Sings

In the garden where silence clings,
You can hear the nightingale sings.
Soft melodies, sweet and low,
Whispers of love, a gentle flow.

Moonlit blooms, their petals gleam,
Dancing lightly in a dream.
The world fades, just you and I,
Beneath the vast, unending sky.

Each note woven with tender care,
A serenade for hearts laid bare.
Where shadows play and spirits soar,
The nightingale opens every door.

In this moment, time stands still,
As we savor each longing thrill.
Here, love blossoms, softly springs,
In the garden where the nightingale sings.

The Hush of Midnight Reveries

In shadows deep, the silence calls,
A gentle whisper through the halls.
Stars wink above, a distant light,
As dreams unfold in velvet night.

The moon reflects on quiet streams,
Where thoughts dance softly, wrapped in dreams.
A sigh escapes, the world stands still,
In midnight's grasp, a silent thrill.

Whispers carried by the breeze,
Kiss the leaves upon the trees.
In the tranquil, still embrace,
I find my heart, a sacred space.

As night drapes all in silver hue,
I chase the thoughts that feel so true.
In hypnotic calm, my spirit soars,
In the hush of night, my soul explores.

Dreams Drift on Aurora's Wings

Beneath the sky, a canvas bright,
Colors swirl in morning's light.
Dreams take flight on swirling beams,
A harmony of whispered dreams.

As dawn awakens, shadows flee,
And all the world begins to see.
Hope ignites in golden streaks,
Each promise born, a fire speaks.

The softest breath of morning's grace,
Embraces all in warm embrace.
With every hue, new stories start,
As auroras paint the dreaming heart.

With wings unbound, my spirit sings,
Embracing life on radiant wings.
In every dawn, a chance reborn,
I rise anew, with hope adorn.

Night's Cauldron of Wonder

In twilight's glow, the magic stirs,
A cauldron brews as evening blurs.
Mystic potions, glimmering bright,
Await the touch of starry night.

Each whisper caught in lunar glow,
A secret too, the shadows know.
With every turn, the world expands,
In night's cauldron, fate commands.

The ancient tales in silence weave,
As mystics dance and hearts believe.
A tapestry of dreams entwined,
In every glance, the unknown find.

The night unfolds, a wondrous stage,
With every beat, a new page.
In this cauldron, fears dissolve,
Where wonders wait, our hearts evolve.

Reflections in the Moonlit Pool

Beneath the stars, the waters gleam,
A mirror of the night's sweet dream.
Each ripple dances with the light,
In whispers soft, the world's delight.

The moon dips low, a silver coin,
Enhancing every shadow's join.
Thoughts drift upon the tranquil tide,
In this embrace, the heart confides.

Night creatures hum a lifting tune,
While crickets serenade the moon.
In quiet depths, my soul takes flight,
A journey spurred by dreams of night.

Reflections twine, a sacred thread,
Connecting what the heart has said.
In moonlit pools, my spirit sees,
The beauty found in gentle ease.

Dreamscapes in Celestial Embrace

In twilight's hue, the stars ignite,
Whispers of dreams take wondrous flight.
Moonlit paths weave tales of old,
In cosmic arms, our hopes unfold.

Clouds of silver, soft and bright,
Carry wishes through the night.
Galaxies dance, a cosmic waltz,
In this embrace, our fears dissolve.

Ethereal tides pull us near,
With every heartbeat, we draw clear.
Lost in visions, time suspended,
In stardust dreams, we are defended.

Beyond the veil, horizons gleam,
Where every star is sewn in dream.
Float on whispers, soar on grace,
In the vastness, find our place.

Lullabies Beneath the Ethereal Glow

Night wraps softly, sweet and deep,
In gentle arms, the world sleeps.
Serenades of stars above,
Weaving peace with threads of love.

Crickets sing in harmony,
A calming chant, a reverie.
Moonlight bathes the earth so light,
In tender dreams, we take flight.

Each sigh a song, each breath a prayer,
In the silence, magic's air.
As night unfolds its velvet bliss,
We find solace in the abyss.

Wrapped in whispers, soft and low,
Drifting where the wild winds blow.
In this embrace, we feel so free,
Lulled by night's sweet symphony.

Journeys through Velvet Skies

Wings unfurl, take to the night,
Through velvet skies, in pure delight.
Stars as guides, they gleam and glow,
Mapping realms we long to know.

With every beat, the heart takes flight,
Into wonders, out of sight.
Clouds like pillows, soft and warm,
Embrace our dreams, shield from harm.

Beneath the dome of cosmic grace,
We find our path in endless space.
Riding winds of silver streams,
Chasing softly whispered dreams.

The universe, a canvas wide,
Where our spirits freely glide.
Journeys forged in starlit streams,
We soar together, lost in dreams.

A Tapestry of Night's Embrace

In twilight's weave, the stars entwine,
A tapestry where dreams align.
Every thread a whispered tale,
Of moonlit paths and winds that sail.

Crimson hues fade into blue,
Where shadows dance and fears renew.
Softly falling, night descends,
In her arms, the journey bends.

Amidst the stars, we find our way,
Threads of silver, bright and gay.
Woven dreams like silken streams,
In night's embrace, we dare to dream.

From cosmic heights to whispered lows,
In every heart, the magic flows.
Together here, we laugh and play,
In night's embrace, we drift away.

Fantasy Adrift on Starlight

Drifting through the skies so wide,
Among the stars, a cosmic ride.
Whispers of worlds, both near and far,
Guided by the light of a silver star.

Oceans of wonder beneath our feet,
Galaxies spinning, a celestial beat.
Imaginations run wild and free,
In this realm of enchantment, we long to be.

Winds of magic swirl around,
Dreams take flight without a sound.
Carried on currents, we lose our way,
In the dance of night, we want to stay.

Never to land on solid ground,
In a starlit cradle, forever bound.
The wonders of space our hearts ignite,
In this fantasy draped in twilight.

The Gauzy Veil of Evening's Embrace

Cascading shadows, the day departs,
A gauzy veil where evening starts.
Whispers ride the gentle breeze,
As twilight weaves through swaying trees.

Soft colors blend into the night,
Stars awaken, a soothing sight.
Crickets sing their timeless tune,
Under the watchful eye of the moon.

Night cloaks the world in deep blue,
A tender hush, a calming view.
Within this embrace, fears fade away,
Under the veil where dreams play.

Hope lingers in twilight's grace,
Each moment wrapped in its warm embrace.
In the fading light, hearts interlace,
With a sigh, we welcome night's face.

Celestial Tides of Serendipity

Waves of stars crash on distant shores,
Whispers carried through cosmic doors.
In the vastness, serendipity glows,
As the universe conspires to show.

Dreams collide in dazzling arcs,
Illuminating the midnight parks.
As comets trace paths across the sky,
We find ourselves soaring high.

Navigating through celestial streams,
Chasing the echoes of our dreams.
Each twinkling light a hope renewed,
In this dance of fate, our spirits brood.

Together we drift on cosmic tides,
In the embrace of the great divides.
With every pulse of the universe bright,
We discover our place in the night.

Night's Cradle of Fanciful Dreams

In the cradle of night, we find our rest,
With stars above, we are truly blessed.
Dreams like clouds drift softly by,
Under the gaze of the midnight sky.

Lullabies sung by the wind's gentle breath,
Filling our hearts with tales of depth.
Imaginary worlds begin to bloom,
In this haven of peace, dispelling gloom.

Each thought a feather, light as air,
Carried on whispers, beyond despair.
Sleep weaves stories in a tender embrace,
Night cradles us in its soft grace.

Awake we shall, with the dawn's first light,
But here, in dreams, we take flight.
In the arms of night, so rich and deep,
We journey through realms before we sleep.

Whims of the Nocturnal Muse

Under the moon's soft, silvery light,
Dreams take flight in the still of the night.
Whispers of shadows dance in the air,
Luring the soul with a tender care.

Stories unwind in the cool, dark embrace,
Each star a tale in the vast, endless space.
Creativity flows like a river anew,
Beneath the gaze of the midnight hue.

Colors unfold in a painter's delight,
Brushstrokes of magic illuminate sight.
A canvas of visions painted with grace,
The muse of the night, a mystical face.

Into the depths where the secrets reside,
Take a bold step, let your heart be your guide.
For every night brings a chance to renew,
In the realm of dreams, where the wondrous ensue.

Twilight's Gentle Calling

As dusk wraps the earth in its velvet embrace,
A hush falls upon with delicate grace.
Colors blend softly, like whispers in song,
Inviting the heart to where shadows belong.

From golden to lavender, hues start to fade,
The dance of the fireflies, a glitter parade.
The sun bows its head, and the stars take their place,
In the hush of the twilight, worries erase.

Gentle winds carry the scent of the night,
While crickets compose their sweet melodies bright.
Each moment a treasure, a spark in the dark,
Twilight speaks softly, igniting the spark.

In this tender hour, let your spirit roam,
For twilight's embrace can feel just like home.
A promise of dreams as you drift and you sway,
In the arms of the night, let the magic hold sway.

Stardust Adventures

In a realm where the cosmos sings bright,
Adventures unfold beneath starlit night.
With each twinkle, a story untold,
A tapestry woven of secrets and gold.

Galaxies swirl in a dance of delight,
Whispers of wonders take rapid flight.
Planets align as our hearts start to race,
Stardust adventures in a limitless space.

Explore the unknown with the cosmos as guide,
Each nebula vibrant, where dreams can reside.
The universe beckons with open embrace,
Inviting the wanderers into the chase.

So rise with the dawn, let the journey commence,
Where stardust adventures ignite the suspense.
With every heartbeat, the magic unfolds,
In the vast, endless sky, your spirit beholds.

Embracing the Enchanted Breeze

A whispering breeze through the branches doth flow,
Carrying secrets only nature can know.
It wraps 'round the heart like a tender embrace,
Inviting the soul to a tranquil space.

The rustle of leaves sings a sweet lullaby,
As the sun dips below the horizon's high.
With each gentle touch, the world comes alive,
In the dance of the dusk, where wishes can thrive.

Cascading like feathers, the soft winds will guide,
Carving paths through the fields where dreams coincide.
In the heart of the moment, our spirits blend,
With the enchanted breeze, where all troubles mend.

So let us surrender to this magical kind,
Where peace is abundant and joy intertwined.
In the embrace of the breeze, we all can be free,
Wandering souls at one with the trees.

Echoes of a Starlit Serenade

In the stillness of the night,
Whispers float on gentle air.
Stars above begin to shine,
Melodies of love laid bare.

Each note dances through the trees,
Painting shadows soft and bright.
Hearts entwined in sweet embrace,
Lost in echoes of delight.

Moonlight casts its silver spell,
As dreams weave through the sky.
In this moment, time stands still,
Together, you and I.

When dawn breaks with golden hues,
Memories linger, warm and clear.
A starlit serenade remains,
Embracing all we hold dear.

Beneath a Canopy of Stars

Lying beneath a vast expanse,
Stars like diamonds flicker bright.
The universe tells its tale,
A symphony of cosmic light.

Whispers of the ancient night,
Guide our dreams on paths unknown.
Each constellation holds a wish,
A magic that feels like home.

In silence, secrets seem to bloom,
While shadows dance with playful glee.
Here, beneath this velvet sky,
We find our hearts are truly free.

So let us drift on stardust waves,
With every breath, a promise made.
Beneath this canopy of stars,
Our love will never fade.

The Quest for Luminous Tranquility

In search of peace, we wander far,
Through valleys deep and mountains high.
With every step, we feel the light,
That leads us beneath the endless sky.

Whispers of the winds embrace,
Guiding us on this serene quest.
The tranquil moments we embrace,
Gift us solace, pure and blessed.

Each glow of dawn brings hope renewed,
As sunbeams touch the waking earth.
In nature's arms, we find our way,
A testament to love's true worth.

We seek the stars in twilight's glow,
A promise of eternal grace.
In the quest for luminous peace,
We've found our rightful place.

Metamorphosis in Celestial Waters

In waters deep, the stars reflect,
A cosmic dance, a vivid show.
Ripples sing of change and growth,
Transformations in ebb and flow.

The moonlight kisses surface clear,
As shadows stretch and play with light.
Each wave a story yet untold,
In tranquil depths, dreams take flight.

Beneath the waves, a world unfolds,
Where colors blend in seamless grace.
In this abyss, we find our truth,
As we behold the vast embrace.

When dawn emerges from the night,
The waters glisten, pure and bright.
In metamorphosis, we soar,
Beneath celestial waters' light.

The Allure of Twilight's Glow

As day bids farewell, the stars arise,
The sky dons hues of deep lilac and rose.
Whispers of evening dance in the breeze,
A moment of magic that time often froze.

Shadows stretch long, in this soft embrace,
The world slows its pulse, surrendering to night.
Moonlight cascades, like a silvery lace,
Painting the landscape in ethereal light.

In the twilight's charm, dreams start to take flight,
Unraveling stories where fantasies blend.
Hearts open wide, longing for the night's might,
In the glow of twilight, all worries can mend.

The allure of dusk, in its tranquil array,
Breathes life into thoughts that linger within.
A whisper, a promise, at the end of the day,
Awakens our souls, and we start to begin.

~eams Drenched in Stardust

In the quiet of night, where wishes take flight,
Only the stars bear witness to dreams.
Soft glimmers of hope blend with shadows so light,
In the dance of the cosmos, nothing is as it seems.

A tapestry woven of whispering glows,
Each particle shimmering, a story to tell.
Floating on stardust, where imagination flows,
The heart sails through galaxies, bidding farewell.

Through nebula clouds, our visions will sweep,
Exploring the realms where the wild spirits roam.
A universe cradles the secrets we keep,
Drenched in the magic that leads us back home.

The beauty of night wraps us in its embrace,
Drenched in the stardust of slumbering dreams.
In the silence of space, we find our safe place,
A haven of comfort where everything gleams.

Illuminations Beneath Galactic Skies

Beneath the vast heavens, where wonders align,
Stars twinkle and beckon, inviting us near.
Galactic displays in their glorious shine,
Illuminate pathways through darkness and fear.

Each pinprick of light tells a tale of its own,
Of journeys unspoken, and moments long past.
In the grand tapestry, our thoughts are sown,
The echoes of ages, forever held fast.

As we gaze into depths, our spirits expand,
Connection to cosmos, a faith we can cling.
In the light of the night, we find our own stand,
Illuminations shining, like celestial strings.

So let us embrace this galactic display,
A reminder that in darkness, there's brilliance to find.
Underneath starlit skies, we're never astray,
With each glowing promise, our souls intertwine.

Secrets Beneath the Midnight Glow

At the edge of twilight, where shadows blend,
Secrets awaken, cloaked in silent grace.
The moon holds its breath, a watchful friend,
Guarding the whispers that time can't erase.

Hidden in darkness, the stories reside,
In the stillness, tales long buried emerge.
Beneath the glow, where fears dare to hide,
Mysteries beckon, like an uncharted surge.

With every heartbeat, the night starts to speak,
Revealing the truths that daylight conceals.
In silence profound, it's hope that we seek,
For the depths of the dark hold the spark that reveals.

So linger awhile, in the midnight's soft hum,
Embrace all the secrets that twilight bestows.
For in every shadow, there's light yet to come,
And beneath the moon's gaze, our true nature grows.

Phosphorescent Trails to Fantasia

In twilight's hush, the lights they gleam,
Phosphorescent dreams, a silent stream.
Footprints glow on paths unknown,
Guiding souls to realms not shown.

Whispers dance on breezes light,
Promises made under the night.
Stars aglow, they flicker bright,
Leading hearts to future's flight.

In realms where magic softly sighs,
Imagination learns to rise.
With every step, the world unfolds,
In colors vivid, tales are told.

Beyond the reach of day's embrace,
A journey born in time and space.
Phosphorescent trails we chase,
As wonder paints our dreams in grace.

Chill of the Midnight Murmurs

When darkness falls and shadows creep,
The midnight murmur stirs from sleep.
A chill runs deep in silenced air,
As secrets weave through twilight's glare.

Echoes whisper, softly sway,
Carrying tales of yesterday.
The moonbeams dance, a ghostly glow,
While ancient winds begin to blow.

In the stillness, hearts can feel,
The hidden truths that shadows steal.
Through whispered winds and rustled leaves,
The night reveals what daylight weaves.

Embrace the chill, the night's allure,
In murmur's depth, our souls are pure.
The echoes beckon, soft and clear,
To journey forth, away from fear.

The Allure of Celestial Journeys

A canvas sprawls in endless vast,
Where dreams and stardust gleam steadfast.
We sail the seas of midnight skies,
With every wish, the cosmos lies.

Galaxies swirl, a cosmic dance,
In twinkling lights, we take our chance.
Each star a beacon, bright and bold,
Whispers of stories yet untold.

In astral realms where wishes bloom,
We chase the light, dispel the gloom.
The universe grants us wings,
As we embrace what adventure brings.

Through constellations, hearts entwined,
In cosmic dreams, our fate aligned.
The allure of journeys waits above,
For seekers bound by stars and love.

Unraveled Secrets of the Night Sky

Secrets swirl in twilight's cloak,
In every star, a story's spoke.
Galaxies twinkle, inviting grace,
Revealing wonders in endless space.

The moon, a watcher, wise and bright,
Casts shadows, guiding through the night.
As constellations weave their tales,
Our souls embark on timeless trails.

Whispers of stardust, soft and sweet,
In the stillness, our hearts can meet.
Through darkened skies, we find our way,
Unraveled dreams in soft array.

In the cosmic dance, we lose our fears,
Embracing the secrets of countless years.
With every glance at night's embrace,
We uncover the magic, the boundless space.

Voyage Into the Midnight Whisper

Upon the sea, the shadows play,
A boat glides softly, night turns day.
Stars reflect on waters deep,
Secrets in the stillness keep.

Waves caress the hull with grace,
Whispers travel, time's embrace.
Guided by the moon's soft light,
Navigators of the night.

Each ripple tells a story old,
Of dreams and hearts, of brave and bold.
In twilight's arms, our spirits soar,
Together bound, forevermore.

To distant shores, we set our sight,
Journey inked in silver light.
Across the vast, uncharted sea,
The midnight calls, we are set free.

Through the Lenses of Dusk

Dusk drapes the sky in hues of gold,
A canvas where dreams unfold.
Shadows dance, embracing the night,
As daylight fades from our sight.

Through lenses dark, we see anew,
A world transformed, vibrant and true.
Whispers of the wind's soft song,
Guide us where we all belong.

Silhouettes of trees rise tall,
In the twilight's tender thrall.
Stars awaken, one by one,
A symphony of night begun.

The horizon blurs, as night descends,
Infinite path where the heart mends.
Through every shade, we find our way,
In the warmth of dusk's embrace, we stay.

The Enchanted Realm of the Night

In whispers soft, the night unfolds,
A realm where magic gently holds.
Mysteries twinkle in the skies,
Where dreams awaken, spirits rise.

Moonlit paths weave through the trees,
As starlight dances on the breeze.
Creatures stir in shadows deep,
In this enchanted realm, we leap.

Each corner hides a tale untold,
Adventures fresh, yet ages old.
We walk among the silent calls,
In twilight's arms, the mystery sprawls.

Beneath the vault of night so grand,
We lose ourselves, hand in hand.
With every heartbeat, futures gleam,
In this enchanted realm, we dream.

Ethereal Riddles in Silver Light

Underneath the moon's soft gaze,
Ethereal riddles weave their maze.
Mystic puzzles softly chime,
In the quiet, lost in time.

Shadows whisper secrets old,
In silver light, the stories unfold.
Each flicker, a tale to tell,
In the silence, where we dwell.

Stars pulse gently, a guiding hand,
Leading us through this twilight land.
With every breath, the night ignites,
In ethereal riddles, our hearts take flight.

The veils of dusk begin to lift,
In this realm, we find our gift.
Eternal echoes softly play,
In silver light, we find our way.

Milton Keynes UK
Ingram Content Group UK Ltd.
UKHW021129021124
450571UK00005B/82